A Salcombe Phot(

C000177859

Images from the col
A E Fairweather

Compiled by Tim Burr and Nicola Fox

© Cookworthy Museum 2008

ORCHARD PUBLICATIONS
2 Orchard Close, Chudleigh, Newton Abbot, Devon TQ13 0LR
Telephone: 01626 852714

ISBN 9781898964865

Printed by Hedgerow Print
Crediton, Devon EX17 1ES

CONTENTS

Acknowledgements

The information and images are taken from the Cookworthy Museum archives. We are particularly grateful to Malcolm Darch and Edward Hannaford for their interest and assistance. However thanks are also due to all the people who have helped to identify photographs from the collection over the years.

Should any reader wish to order a photo from this collection please contact the Cookworthy Museum, 108 Fore Street, Kingsbridge TQ7 1AW, quoting the page number and caption.

INTRODUCTION

The name of Fairweather is well known in Salcombe, and to many it can immediately be associated with photography and the many photographs of Salcombe and its people produced by A E Fairweather in the first half of the 20th century.

Alfred Edward Fairweather (1876-1959) was one of the four sons of James Fairweather, a prominent local businessman active in community affairs and the Methodist Church. James Fairweather ran a printing and stationery business in Salcombe for many years, later including the publication of local newspapers. He also produced a local guide, *Salcombe and Neighbourhood, a Descriptive and Historical Guide to all places of interest between Start Bay and the River Avon*, first published in 1884.

Alfred did not follow his father into the printing trade: he was originally apprenticed to a pharmacist in Kingsbridge and trained at Stewarts, Dispensing Chemists, at 56 Fore Street. However he did not complete his training, instead teaching himself photography, and set up his own business in about 1900. His studio was in Robinsons Row in Salcombe, to the rear of his father's business at 67 Fore Street. He would walk long distances with his heavy camera and equipment in search of a good picture, then develop and print his own photographs of events, people and places in the town.

He also published postcards of local views, and his advertisement in a later edition of *Salcombe and Neighbourhood* describes him as a portrait and landscape photographer and photographic dealer. Some negatives were purchased from other businesses, for example Balley and Flower of Kingsbridge, whose records went back to the late 19th century, and Mrs. Haynes. Fairweather postcards were widely distributed and continue to be valued by those who possess copies: and there also seems to have been a steady trade in studio portraits of local people.

By 1926 Alfred had set up his own shop at 8 Fore Street, which he ran until it was damaged by enemy action in 1943. He had prided himself on never destroying a negative, but this raid destroyed much of his stock although friends and neighbours helped him to rescue as many negatives and plates as they could.

J A L (Len) Fairweather, Alfred's son, also took an interest in photography, helping part-time in the shop, and inherited his father's collection of plates and negatives. He continued the family tradition of writing about local history and collaborated in the production of several books of photographs about Salcombe, Kingsbridge and the area. Following his death in 1990, the collection was donated to the Cookworthy Museum in Kingsbridge.

The images in this book are all taken from the Fairweather Collection at the Cookworthy Museum, reproduced from original negatives or earlier glass plates, and depict a variety of local scenes and events in the first half of the 20th century. Most of them were taken in the period 1900 – 1940, although there are some with earlier dates which appear to have come from other collections purchased. Some have their own captions with specific dates and some can be linked to local or national events, but others cannot be pinned down precisely. The intention is not to provide a detailed history but to make these wonderful photographs available to a wider audience.

The surviving collection provides an unique record, rich in detail, of Salcombe life over nearly half a century. There are postcard views, portraits, pictures of the town in all its aspects, celebrations, work, the sea and the lifeboats as essential parts of the town's life, news items, action shots and weather conditions. Some of them appear a little stiff to a modern eye – hardly any wonder, with the length of exposure required for earlier shots. Some show the frank curiosity and sometimes slight suspicion, of the subjects, watching the photographer at work while being recorded themselves. They are taken from wherever was the best vantage point – on boats, using the height of nearby buildings, whatever was needed to get the best picture – but they are still composed with the same skilled eye, and the clarity of detail reveals more the closer you look at them.

Alfred Fairweather thoroughly deserves his reputation in Salcombe and further afield and we hope this book will enhance that reputation. We also hope that you will enjoy reading it as much as we have enjoyed working on it.

Equipment used

Alfred Fairweather and his contemporaries would have typically used a half plate folding camera fitted with one of several lenses such as an Aldis No 8, 9 inch focal length with aperture settings from F7.7 to F45 and mounted on a focal plane shutter providing preset shutter speeds of 1/15 to 1/90 and bulb setting.

Being very cumbersome to carry and time consuming to set up this would comprise firstly, the baseboard equipped with an integral turntable into which the tripod legs fitted, secondly, the lens panel pivoted to allow the camera to fold closed and provide more versatility of use and thirdly, a double rack and pinion assembly to aid movements and convenience when focussing under a dark cloth.

PEOPLE

South Pool Harriers meet at Portlemouth.

Boatman under Harry Cook's quay, possibly one of the Cook family.

Banana growing at Sharpitor, Salcombe, with small child in the foreground to provide scale. The gardens at Sharpitor are still noted for their range of tender and sub-tropical plants, which continues to include bananas.

Catching a shark in the harbour merited public display and this one is seen on Harry Cook's quay in 1906. The bystanders include (on the left) Alban Pepperell, a shipsmith, and Aaron Dornom, junior. Ashley and Florence Cook are the two children sitting on a canoe.

Fish market at Salcombe, on what is now Whitestrand Quay, after a particularly large catch had been landed.

Isaac Jarvis and Jack Argeat, Hope Cove fishermen and lifeboatmen, instrumental in rescuing survivors from the Jebba in March 1907.

A practice launch of the Salcombe lifeboat Lesty from the Lifeboat House at South Sands, c 1900.

Lifeboat Day, August 5th 1922. Then, as now, the lifeboat service relied on donations. Fundraisers are seen at Whitestrand, with the Sarah Anne Holden and crew behind them.

KING GEORGE V SILVER JUBILEE MAY 6ᵗʰ 1935. SALCOMBE

Fore Street in Salcombe, decorated to celebrate the Silver Jubilee of King George V in May 1935.

More decorations for King George V's Silver Jubilee, this time at the top of Robinsons Row. On the left are Jack Damerell, Bettine Hobbs, Thelma Patey and Cyril Patey – and the dog was called Nancy!

Maypole dancers, Salcombe, 1904.

Large crowd on Church Hill, Salcombe, during the First World War.

Large group of children dressed in their best and accompanying adults, at the end of Island Street on the boatyard site. The occasion is the Wesleyan Methodist Sunday School Anniversary, on Whit Monday 1914.

Salcombe section Devon RGA, drivers exercising, c 1908. The Devonshire Royal Garrison Artillery were a territorial force. No. 2 Heavy Battery was based at Devonport with drill stations at Plymouth and Salcombe. The headquarters and units moved to Plymouth as part of defences of the Port of Plymouth during the First World War, but were not deployed overseas.

Salcombe Royal Fleet Reserves and pensioners leaving for active service during the First World War, with a crowd in Fore Street to give them a suitable send-off. They are the five men in uniform, with individual captions: LS Stagg, Chief Stoker Dimond, Gunner T. Canham, CPO Wood, S... Cossentine. The waiting GWR bus behind them would have taken them to the railway station at Kingsbridge.

Vessels moored and moving in the harbour during Salcombe Regatta week. There seems to be a very heavy crop of seaweed on the Portlemouth side of the estuary.

Salcombe Regatta 1925. During the annual Regatta an area off Victoria Quay was roped off for swimming races and watersports and spectators could either stay on dry land or watch from boats on the seaward edge of the area, as shown. The row of lads on the right are sitting on a cargo of bricks which had been unloaded at the quay. Note the almost universal wearing of hats among the crowd.

Salcombe Carnival, April 24th 1924. Charlie Chaplin and a Pierrot with his accordion entertaining young bystanders in Fore Street, Salcombe.

Salcombe Carnival, April 24th 1924. A group of carnival entrants in Devon Road waiting to move off.

Salcombe Carnival August 1925. Four elegant ladies portraying 'The Latest from Paris'.

Salcombe Carnival August 1925. A new form of advertising!

Spectators at the Regatta in 1920, occupying every available foot of Victoria Quay.

Salcombe Regatta watersports in 1925, with spectators afloat. Portlemouth in the background.

An exhibition with visitors, probably at the Methodist Church in Island Street.

Group of six gentlemen at the thatched shelter which stood under the cliffs on the north side of North Sands beach. It was known locally as the 'Monkey House' and was destroyed in the 1950s after a tree fell on it.

Three men and a dog on the site of Vivian's, later Chant's yard on the Salcombe waterfront.

Prawning in Salcombe Harbour at low tide, with Ilbertstow (Snapes Point) in the background.

Salcombe Rugby Football Club Annual Dinner, Cliff House, Salcombe, 20th May 1948. Eddie Burner, whose family owned the Victoria Inn for many years, is 3rd from right in the front row.

Site of the 'new' Salcombe Wesleyan Church, with volunteers at work and appeal for funds. The church on the Allenhayes Road site was opened in 1928.

Jim Stone, later a well-known boatbuilder and his Regatta rowing trophies.

A horse and carriage waiting in the road outside the Square at Inner Hope. The lady on the far left is Mrs Alfred Fairweather.

Street scene in Island Street, looking towards Ilbertstow. The bystanders include a sailor in uniform and a street sweeper.

Mrs. Forbes' 90th birthday party at the Salcombe Sisterhood, April 5th 1937. The Sisterhood was the ladies' meeting attached to the Methodist Church and they are seen here in the Methodist Schoolroom. Again, the wearing of hats is almost universal.

Street decorations for the Silver Jubilee of George V, May 1935. The Town Hall, on the left, was used for a variety of purposes and was converted into a cinema in 1931. The hall and cottages were demolished for road widening in the 1960s.

INDUSTRY

Fishing boats were hauled up over the beach at Beesands when they came in from sea and everyone available was expected to lend a hand.

The head of the estuary at Kingsbridge in the 1920s, with the Promenade on the left and the timberyard buildings on the right, below Quay House. There are two local barges used for cargo work in the harbour, alongside the quay, and a ketch aground in the middle of the picture.

The Express alongside New Quay, from the opposite shore at Tacket Wood. The Express was a wooden paddle steamer built at Date's Yard in Kingsbridge, launched in 1885: she had to be modified soon after her launch as she was too buoyant and her paddles did not touch the water.

The Express and a sailing vessel alongside New Quay, Kingsbridge, where a great deal of the town's shipping trade came in. The quay and the New Quay Inn were owned by the Bond family, as were the barns and stores to the left of the picture.

One of the Great Western Railway buses which provided a connection from Salcombe to the railway at Kingsbridge.

Donkey and cart travelling the road above Fishermans Cove.

An example of Brenton's Prize Seed Drill, manufactured by W. Brenton of St. Germans', Cornwall.

Pitts & Bucknell engine and thresher, owned by W. Yabsley of Goodshelter, one of the largest local contractors. The threshing machinery and team would work their way around the area, as very few farmers had their own threshers.

Workmen on Salcombe gasometer. Note the spectators at window! The Salcombe gasworks, in Gould Road, were first opened in 1866.

TWO TONS MULLETT CAUGHT AT SALCOMBE VC 29

A record catch of two tons of mullet being boxed up for sale on Tommy Elliott's quay along Island Street.

Local accidents were also of interest to a photographer and this is one of a series of pictures of a steamroller crash in the Plantation, below Devon Road in Salcombe, in 1928. The steamroller belonged to W. Burgoyne of Kingsbridge and is seen in its damaged state with the roller missing and an audience of interested small boys.

The steamroller was salvaged by using two traction engines to haul it up the bank. This picture shows Burgoyne's traction engine 'Lord Kitchener' in the foreground, driven by Bill Elliott with Mr. Alfred Burgoyne (in the trilby) co-ordinating operations.

Continuing salvage operations, shown from the reverse angle.

The damaged vehicle, with the roller at a distance. Apart from the boy posing on top of the roller, there are several others in the undergrowth.

The story is that the man driving the steamroller was one Harry Trute, who had misjudged his machine and gone over the edge of the road during his dinner hour. His workmates raised a cry of 'Harry's dead!', but fortunately he was very much alive and replied 'No I bain't, where's me 'at?'

Aaron Dornom, senior, and his apprentices at work, c. 1901. L to R: Weymouth Johnson, Aaron's son Wilfred, Edgar Cove, Fred Heath and Frederic Murch. Dornom's yard can be seen in the picture on page 39.

Edwin (Ned) Stone watching his five grandchildren playing in a pot, near Small's Cove, Portlemouth. Ned Stone was an expert basket and crab-pot maker.

The Effort loading at New (Bond's) Quay, Kingsbridge. The Effort was an 85 ton ketch, built by William Date at Kingsbridge in 1880. Those with shares in the vessel were all Kingsbridge and Salcombe men, including the builder and Edison Lapthorne, master mariner and captain, of Salcombe. The gentleman in the boater is William Bond with Captain Lapthorne in a peaked cap with a bobble to his left.

Old House, Fore Street, Salcombe. The entrance to King's Arms Quay is on the left. Several of the buildings in this area were condemned in the 1930s and when the American forces were stationed in Salcombe in the 1940s they were cleared for better access to the harbour, leaving a space which is today's Whitestrand car park.

Ellis's Grocery, Fore Street, Salcombe. Note the cobbled pavement and the handcart in the side alley, probably for local deliveries.

An unusual sight, a working boat being poled through ice on the frozen estuary, possibly near Gerston. This appears to be one of the older photographs in the collection and could be one of those acquired from Mrs. Haynes of Kingsbridge, relating to the Great Blizzard of 1891.

MARITIME

View of the northern end of Salcombe, taken from Ilbertstow (now Snapes Point). Edgar Cove's boatyard is visible in the foreground and behind it the Wesleyan Chapel, both now demolished. The lines of washing would seem to indicate that it is a Monday.

The Ilton Castle leaving Custom House or Steamer Quay. A tops'l schooner can be seen alongside the quay in the background. There were regular passenger and goods services by paddle steamer between Salcombe, Kingsbridge and Plymouth.

Customs Quay on a calm day, c 1920, with resident swans

View of Salcombe Harbour, c 1908, showing vessels moored in the harbour. Among them are the ketches Shortest Day and Eclipse and the barges Yealm, Phoenix, Emma and J.N.R.

View of Salcombe in August 1899, showing Holy Trinity Church, the Wesleyan Chapel and 'Bethel Steps', with Island House to the right of the picture. The ketch rigged vessel in the foreground is lying at Harnden's Yard — note the crewman sitting on the bowsprit.

Council Quay, Salcombe, c 1908, with the site of Dornom's Yard to the right. The man with the basket is Pilot Robert Foale and Florence Cook is the little girl in the pinafore.

J Class racing off the Ferry Hard, Portlemouth, in the late 1930s. Juanita is the furthest from the camera, the first Wiluna A4 is next and Albert 'Flannel' Pepperell, a noted helmsman, is nearest the ferry hard in the Joan. Captain Southwood, the harbourmaster, is standing in the dinghy.

The yacht 'Goshawk', built in 1865 by Hansen of Cowes, crossing the Bar in 1908 and towing the pilot boat. Tennyson's well-known poem 'Crossing the Bar' is reputed to have been inspired by Salcombe Harbour and its Bar.

Yachts in Salcombe Harbour on a particularly low tide. The bunting indicates that it is probably Regatta Week in August.

An early photograph taken outside 'The Grange', looking back up the harbour, dated 1896. The wall on the right of the road was above head height in those days, before the road was widened and Cliff House gardens were landscaped and opened to the public. The 3-masted barquentine Gaerwen is moored in midstream and the Watch House on the waterfront was occupied by the Coastguard.

A general view of Salcombe in the late 1930s.

Salcombe waterfront, looking upstream towards Custom House Quay. Taken from Chant's yard, showing Chapman's Quay, Cooks Boathouse and Dornoms' Yard with the large corrugated iron roof.

The Quays from Custom House Quay, Salcombe, c 1904, on a working day, with sacks of goods ready to be moved. Further downstream, a topsail schooner is alongside Kings Arms Quay.

Dates Yard, Kingsbridge viewed from Tacket Wood. John Jordain and Henry Martin were earlier shipbuilders on this site, but William Date is recorded as launching his first vessel in 1847 and he and his family continued to operate the shipyard until the early 20th century. The site is now occupied by 'The Moorings', a modern residential development.

The Kenwith Castle, another of the estuary steamers, fully loaded with passengers. She came into service in May 1914 and this could well be her maiden voyage.

Launch of the Joan, one of the J Class keel racers (reference to J Class - page 37) from the Chadder Blank boatyard in 1921. Alf Chadder Blank (the builder) is seen behind the bow of the boat. The Joan was more recently restored and relaunched by her current owner, Mr. Pat Newberry, in August 2005.

'After the Storm' showing the wreck of the Elder Dempster liner Jebba, which ran ashore near Bolt Tail on March 18th 1907. The salvage vessel in the background is the Elcho Castle belonging to 'Wrecker' Distin of Salcombe.

The schooner Ensign wrecked on the Blackstone Rock in Salcombe Harbour, January 30th 1915. She had been attempting to enter the harbour without a pilot and sank very quickly, leaving only the tops of the rigging above water. Her cargo of coal was washed ashore at North Sands and traces of it could be seen in the sand for many years.

A well-known wreck in the area, the Finnish barque Herzogin Cecilie ran on to the Ham Stone off Soar Mill Cove on 25th April 1936. The Salcombe lifeboat Alfred & Clara Heath took off twenty-one of the crew members and one passenger, returning later for the remainder. Attempts were made to save her by bringing her into Starehole Bay and removing her cargo of wheat, but they were ultimately unsuccessful.

The Herzogin Cecilie, ashore in fog at Soar Mill Cove, seen on the morning of the wreck.

A later picture of the Herzogin Cecilie in Starehole Bay. Note the canvas ventilators, which were fitted to remove the gases from the cargo of wheat.

The Jane Rowe, a Swedish steamship which went ashore below Bolberry Down on 28th February 1914. Attempts were made to refloat her, but by the following day she was broadside on to the cliff and the crew were rescued by the coastguard with rocket apparatus.

The tug *Joffre* ashore on rocks below *Bolberry Down. She was built for the Lawson Steamboat Company of Newcastle in 1916 and was wrecked in 1925 on her way from Falmouth to Antwerp. Lifeboatman Jack Jarvis of Hope Cove, son of Isaac Jarvis of Jebba fame (see page 42), was awarded the Board of Trade Bronze Medal for gallantry in saving life at sea for his part in assisting the Joffre.*

COAST SCENE NEAR HOPE (WRECK JOFFRE) No. 4.

WRECK "JOFFRE" AT SALCOMBE – SALVED – JUNE 18th 1925. No.7

The Joffre was salvaged and towed into Millbay in June 1925, by the Trover of the Liverpool Salvage Association. She eventually went to the breakers' yard in 1966.

The Salcombe lifeboat Sarah Anne Holden. She replaced the William and Emma, which capsized on the Bar at Salcombe drowning thirteen of her crew on 27th October 1916. Edwin Distin, one of the two survivors of the disaster, became coxswain of the new lifeboat.

The naming ceremony for the Salcombe lifeboat Samuel and Marie Parkhouse, Cliff House Gardens, 1938. She continued in service at Salcombe until October 1962.

Lifeboat crew members on board the Alfred and Clara Heath in the 1930s: Back row, L to R: Philip Chant, Eddie Distin (coxswain), Gerald Shepherd, Edwin Chant (seated). Front row, L to R: Jack Field, Bill Spry, Billy Didcot, William Jarvis. Foreground: John Allen (mechanic). The woollen hoods were knitted by local supporters.

The Salcombe Castle leaving Salcombe, c 1910. As well as the regular steamer services, excursions to various destinations were also available.

The Brizo at anchor in Salcombe Harbour, c 1885. She was built in Vivian's yard at Salcombe in 1877 and was wrecked on Samphire Cay in the Bahamas in 1886, with no loss of life.

PLACES

A snowy Christmas at Salcombe in 1906.

Looking down on Salcombe from Onslow Road. A very similar viewpoint to the 1906 snow scene, but a different season. Coronation Road, still relatively new, can be seen on the left. The allotments in the centre belonged to the Salcombe Hotel, supplying their vegetables.

Salcombe was originally part of the parish of Malborough and Holy Trinity Church was not in operation until 1844. There was a small cemetery attached to the church, but Shadycombe Cemetery was opened in the 1870s when this proved insufficient. This is an unusual view from the top of Shadycombe Cemetery across to the church and the harbour beyond.

A more distant view of Holy Trinity Church, with Portlemouth in the background.

Millbay beach from the other side of the harbour. As well as increased development, there has been a considerable build-up of sand on the beach during the 20th century.

The head of Batson Creek and the Green in 1927. The small boy has been identified as Len Fairweather, the son of A E Fairweather, aged about fourteen.

Postcard picture of Portlemouth and Salcombe Harbour. Part of Alfred Fairweather's business involved taking views for postcards, either for sale himself or for use by other companies.

Another typical local view, of rough weather at North Sands beach.

The head of the creek and bridge at South Pool. Again a single figure of a small girl has been used to give scale.

Cottages at Gullet, South Pool. The construction of the present large private house began in 1925.

Outer Hope viewed from above Mouthwell Beach in 1880.

The main street in Thurlestone, a little below the Buckland turning. Unaccompanied cattle are obviously nothing unusual.

The Gara Rock Hotel, converted from a row of coastguard cottages above Rickham Sands, seen here in its early years as a boarding house with a maid serving tea on the lawn.

The Gara Rock Hotel c 1930, completely altered from the original cottages. The hotel underwent a number of further changes and was demolished for redevelopment in the early 21st century.

Hallsands, tucked under the cliffs, was always likely to be vulnerable to the sea. Following the dredging of the Skerries Bank and the removal of shingle from Start Bay, the village was almost completely destroyed in 1917. This picture shows Hallsands village in 1902, with early sea walls in place.

Viewing storm damage at Hallsands, c. 1904.

Villagers at Hallsands demonstrating the various stages in the making of crab pots.

Hallsands village looking north, c 1910

Beesands, viewed from the cliff above. At this angle the beach appears almost flat, covered with washing lines, boats and fishing equipment.

Lower Road, Galmpton.

Corner Stores, 7 Fore Street, Kingsbridge. The entrance to the Foundry (destroyed by enemy action in World War II) can be seen in the background along Duke Street.

Island House and Ebrington Street, Kingsbridge, from the bottom of Church Street. Island House was replaced by the Regal Cinema, which in turn became a bingo hall and the Regal Social Club.

The 'King of Prussia' and the turnings to Duke Street and Bridge Street in Kingsbridge. Enemy action in 1943 destroyed much of both these streets, including Lidstone's Foundry.

The higher part of Church Street, outside the Phoenix Brewery (on the left of picture), c 1900. 4th from right is George Rundle, who worked in the brewery for the Kelland family.

The head of the estuary at Kingsbridge, pre-1921. The Town Mill is working, as can be seen by the plume of smoke and there is a paddle-steamer at the quayside.

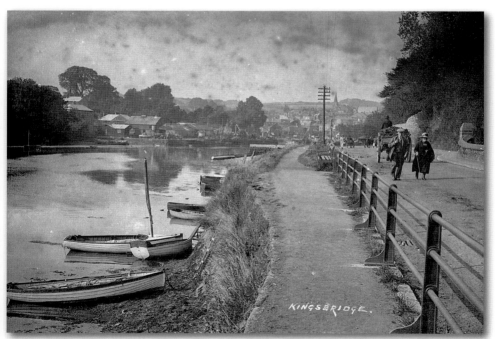

A view along the estuary at Kingsbridge towards the town, just below the present turning to Waterside Park. The timberyard buildings can be seen on the left bank, between the bottom of Tumbly Hill and the town.

Another postcard view of cottages in South Milton, with the church in the background.

Looking down the main street of Bantham from an unusual angle, with the Sloop Inn and patrons on the left.

Cottages in Bigbury, including Post Office

Cottages near the top of Shute Hill in Lower Town, Malborough, with passers-by.

East Portlemouth village street, with Salcombe town in the background.

A typical village store at Kellaton, with the owner and family suitably posed.

Salcombe Harbour and water traffic. Note the shaly beach of Fisherman's Cove in the foreground – the sand which attracts today's visitors built up later in the 20th century.

Clifton Place in Salcombe, next to the slipway at Chapel End.

View up the Bag towards Kingsbridge, from above Ditch End. Two steamers visible, one towing a sailing vessel. The vessel in the foreground has been identified as the yacht, Rose of Devon.

Fore Street, Salcombe, looking towards the Union Inn (now the Fortescue) and the steps up to Buckley Street.

Street scene in Fore Street, Salcombe, c 1904. The large double-fronted shop in the centre background, beyond the Temperance Hotel, is that of James Fairweather, Alfred's father, who is listed in Kelly's Directory of 1906 as a printer and newspaper proprietor at 67 Fore Street.

Courtenay Street, Salcombe. On left side of street Fanny May and Katie May (dressmaker) and unknown girl. On right side of street unknown woman and child, the widow of Captain May, the widow of Mr. Care (drowned) and Mrs. Adams (captain's wife).

'Crowder Cottage' or 'John Hart's Cottage' below the church was thought to have Tudor or earlier origins. Note the steps cut across the steep part of the street.

Another picture of the same subject at a later date, simply captioned 'Old House and Church, Salcombe'.

Coronation Road, Salcombe. Built c 1905 on the site of an orchard.

Street scene in Island Street. The refuse cart, drawn by 'Prince', called twice a week.

Cottages in Victoria Place, behind Breakwater Bay. Notice the outside WCs and wash-houses across the courtyard. The cottages were badly damaged in World War II and the area redeveloped, now the site of the Salcombe Day Centre.

Another view of the Union Inn, now the Fortescue, this time looking up towards Buckley Street and Lee Mount.

The Custom House, Salcombe – an important establishment in this seafaring town. The foundation stone was laid in 1847 and the Custom House continues in use today.

The seaward end of Union Street and the Custom House.

Market Street, Salcombe. Two delivery men with ponies, outside the butcher's shop in Chapel End. This area of Salcombe was one of those damaged by enemy action in 1943.

High tide causing flooding in the lower part of Fore Street.

Fore Street, Salcombe, c 1900. The shops include those of Alfred Cook, the fishmonger, seen on the left holding a crab.

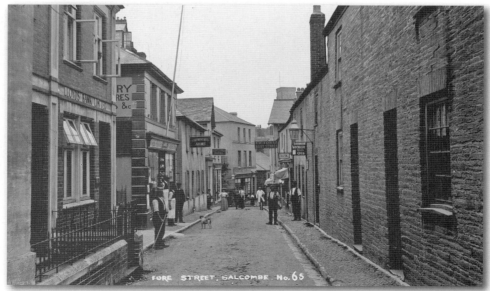

Street scene in Fore Street, Salcombe. The Lloyds Bank building on the left is little changed, and the lines of the buildings are still similar today, although most of the other businesses are long gone.

Ferry Corner in Fore Street, with the sign and steps to the ferry and Ferry Inn on the left.

Group of children in Island Street, at the junction outside the Wesleyan Chapel. There is a ghost image of a hand in the right foreground, which may well be the photographers.

These workmen's cottages in Caroline Place, Shadycombe were built for about £20 each.

Caroline Place viewed from the reverse angle. This time the photographer is standing outside 'Rose Cottage' at the foot of Shadycombe Hill.

The upper end of Fore Street, Salcombe outside the Salcombe (York) Hotel.

Bakers Well Cottages, looking towards the Marine Hotel.

The Moult, Salcombe. The first of the 'villas' to be built in the town, in 1765. Later the home of the eminent Victorian historian J A Froude (1818-94).

BOLT HEAD TEA GARDENS SALCOMBE. No. 119

The Tea Gardens above South Sands. The gentleman standing on the left is Mr. James Fairweather, the photographer's father.

An early photograph of South Sands, showing the lifeboat house almost alone on the sea front. The lifeboat house was built in 1870, at a cost of £309 10s. Salcombe Castle or Fort Charles can also be seen in the background.

Shadycombe Creek, Salcombe in about 1910, viewed from the north side. The Island Street shore has been built up considerably over the 20th century.